The Jesus Boat

Jim Reimann

Illustrations by Najwan Zoubi

Yuval and Moshe lived by the Sea of Galilee,

And were Jewish fishermen, just like their dad.

They'd always believed a great gift would come from the sea,

And one day it happened, which made them quite glad.

It was in 1986, that it came to pass,

Walking by the sea they came upon a truck.

It was sitting on the seashore, but not out of gas;

Its wheels were deep in the mud—completely stuck.

As the wheels of the truck spun more and more to get free,

The brothers saw old coins flung from the earth.

The two gathered these ancient treasures from Galilee,

But underneath was something of greater worth.

The brothers dug some more, and Roman nails were soon mined,

Along with several large pieces of wood.

And when the scientists came to confirm their great find,

A double rainbow shone above where they stood!

Yuval and Moshe, seeing this true sign from the Lord,

Knew this must be more than just sticks in the mud;

It was an ancient fishing boat—not just any board—

Yet was stuck onshore by an earlier flood.

The two fishermen, with others, continued to dig,

Uncovering a boat two thousand years old.

They soon knew this discovery was a find quite big—

A boat from Jesus' day—something to behold!

After much hard digging, the boat was finally free,

Then soaked in a bath to harden its soft wood.

At last, now placed in a museum for all to see,

It tells a story—one that is true and good.

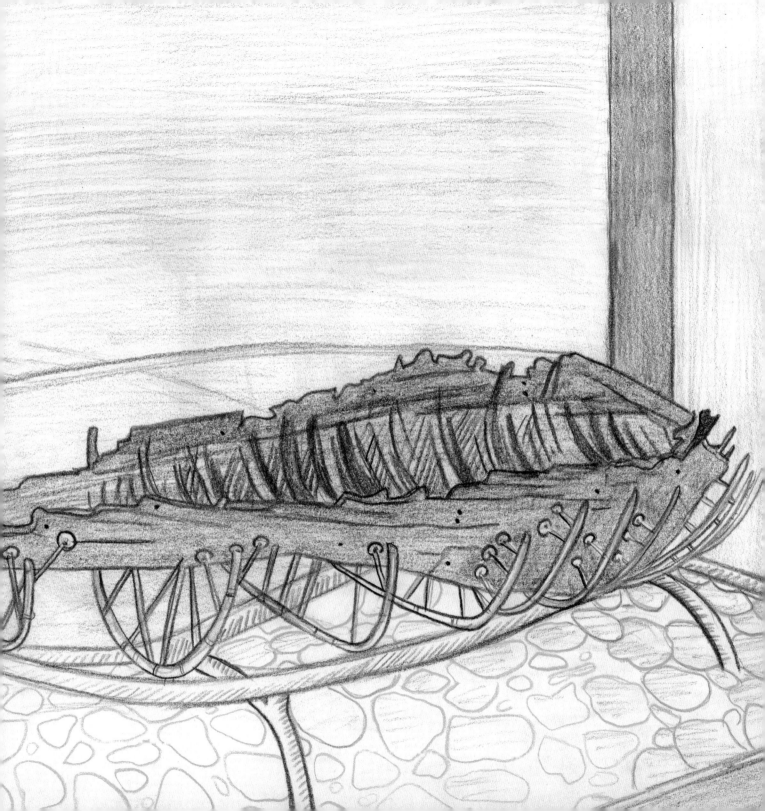

It was in a boat much like this ancient one, we know

Jesus and His friends sailed out one night—until:

A furious, strong storm arose and began to blow,

Yet Jesus calmed it, by saying, "Peace, be still!"

Jesus' friends saw the miraculous end of the storm,

But were asked by Him, "Why are you still afraid?"

They had seen a miracle, their mighty Lord perform,

Yet asked, "Who is this—Whom wind and waves obeyed?"

Still today, some ask, "Who is this Man who calmed the sea?"

Perhaps a question some may find strange or odd;

But it is not a mystery for you, or for me:

He is the Savior! The Messiah of God!

The Ancient Galilee Boat, also known as "The Jesus Boat," is exhibited at the Yigal Allon Center at the Ginosar Kibbutz by the shores of the Sea of Galilee near Capernaum.

Email: mail@JesusBoat.com
Tel: 97246712073, ext. 4
www.JesusBoat.com

This model represnts what
"The Jesus Boat"
may have looked like 2,000 years ago,
based on the most reliable historical
and archaeological evidence.

Rev. Jim Reimann
Israel Tour Leader of 25+ Pilgrimages
Editor of the Updated Editions of:
My Utmost for His Highest (Oswald Chambers)
Streams in the Desert (Lettie Cowman)
Morning by Morning (Charles Spurgeon)
Evening by Evening (Charles Spurgeon)

ISBN: 978-965-7607-08-4

For ordering information, please contact the publisher:

Intelecty, Ltd.
76 Hagalil
Nofit, Israel 36001
Tel: 97249930922
Fax: 972722830147
Mobile: 972523348598
amirarkind@gmail.com

Printed by **GESTELIT**
info@gestelit.co.il

Printed in the Holy Land